The Creative Classroom

Liz Webster and Sue Reed

10.2012

Acknowledgements

Liz Webster and Sue Reed would like to thank all the members of Aldingbourne art club, who produced lots of our fantastic art work.

An enormous thank-you must go to Wendy Davies and Kath Herbert for their hard work and dedication in helping us create such fantastic displays. We don't know what we'd do without you!

A special thanks to Steve and Alison Forrest who have made some very long photo shoots seem incredibly easy!

Finally, we would like to say thanks to Dominic Gasson for his superb IT support – you are a star*!

The whole book has been a pleasure to write and thanks to HarperCollins for giving us the opportunity to write such a great book!

Published by Collins
An imprint of HarperCollins*Publishers*
77–85 Fulham Palace Road
Hammersmith
London
W6 8JB

© HarperCollins*Publishers* Limited 2012

10 9 8 7 6 5 4 3 2 1

ISBN-13 978 0 00 747239 0

Liz Webster and Sue Reed assert their moral rights to be identified as the authors of this work.

British Library Cataloguing in Publication Data
A Catalogue record for this publication is available from the British Library

Cover concept by Mount Deluxe
Inside cover design by Neil Adams
Edited by Alison Sage

Internal design and cover design by Lodestone Publishing Limited
Photography by Elmcroft Studios
Proofread by Gaynor Spry

Printed and bound by Printing Express Limited, Hong Kong

Browse the complete Collins catalogue at
www.collinseducation.com

MIX
Paper from
responsible sources
FSC C007454
FSC
www.fsc.org

372
110
2
web

Contents

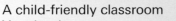

Introduction

In this book, we would like to share some of the discoveries we have made setting up and managing our classrooms. We hope that we can suggest ways to make this task exciting and full of possibilities. This book is aimed both at newly qualified teachers who might be wondering about the best way to approach a new, empty classroom, and also to experienced teachers looking for fresh ideas.

In each chapter, we aim to cover an aspect of good classroom practice – and to extend it beyond the classroom into the playground. However, it goes without saying that the best teaching practice is when teachers, parents, carers and children work together to create a safe, purposeful and happy atmosphere.

1 Organising your Classroom
At the beginning of a new school year, there is always a feeling of excitement, anticipation and maybe also a little flutter of apprehension if you are taking over a new, empty classroom. Here we suggest ways to set up your classroom and make it child-friendly and welcoming. We believe that underpinning everything should be organisation – plus creativity!

2 Managing your Classroom
This chapter offers you a range of practical suggestions to help make your classroom an effective environment, including ways to group children, rules and rewards, and target setting. The sense of achievement when it is all functioning as it should is fantastic.

3 Display in your Classroom

We discuss from start to finish how to create useful and exciting displays (which are never wallpaper!) celebrating children's work and learning, together with tips for putting up functional and information displays.

4 Resourcing your Classroom

Stimulating resources can turn a good lesson into a brilliant one and can make the most ordinary classroom items fun. We describe resources that you can buy or make which will be worth their weight in gold, from pencil pots to giant egg timers.

5 Teaching in your Classroom

Once your classroom is established there is only one more thing left to do… **teach**! This chapter includes a wealth of ideas to help to make your teaching creative and dynamic including games, using puppets and teaching in role.

6 Outside your Classroom

Teaching does not just happen inside the classroom. It is important to make use of all the available space within your school. This chapter includes imaginative ideas for extending your teaching beyond the classroom, such as role play areas and new ways to use the playground for lessons.

This is a book of suggestions and strategies that can be applied to any age range. Every idea in this book has been tried and tested in our own classrooms and when put together, should help to make your classroom the perfect place for a child to develop life-long habits of learning.

We hope you have as much fun in your classroom as we do, every day!

Liz Webster and Sue Reed

Organising your Classroom

The welcome factor

An essential part of teaching, whether you are experienced or newly qualified, is creating a classroom with the 'welcome' factor. It should seem an exciting and purposeful place to be. Children need to feel safe and secure in an environment that promises a fun-filled approach to learning. Your classroom should be child-friendly, organised, bright and colourful. The minute a child, adult or visitor enters the classroom they should know who's who and what's what.

Meet the team

This display shows the members of the team working in the classroom with clearly-named photographs of each person.

1   Decide on a colour scheme. It's best to use a maximum of two or three colours, to make a striking effect.

2   Create a large title: for example, *Meet the Team*, and take a photo of each team member – a head shot is best. It is vital that these are nice and big and very smiley!

3   Label each team member with their name. Again, make sure these labels are big and very visible. Add decoration, like spots or stars, for a lively, jolly effect.

Welcome to the reception class

This display is about welcoming children by showing them photos of all the fun things that they can hope to experience while they are in your class. At the beginning of the year, these photographs should be of past pupils, but as the year progresses, the teacher replaces them with images of the current class.

1   As this is a permanent display, it is best not to take up a valuable display board for the entire year, but to use a wall that otherwise would be a blank area. The display here has been created using the teacher's cupboard door and wall. This is a very good use of classroom space and helps to make a dull area look colourful and vibrant.

2   Decide on a colour scheme. Create lettering that spells: 'Welcome to the Reception Class'. Here we have added an extra title: 'It's a special little world'.

3   Take photographs of children at work and play, showing off as many aspects of school life as possible. Print these out nice and big, and back on an appropriate colour. If this is in a high-traffic area in your classroom, it is a good idea to laminate the photos so they stay looking good. There is nothing worse than dog-eared, tatty displays that stay up all year.

4   Add silver stars to create a magical effect!

Further ideas

- Brighten up your classroom door with a class photo and a welcoming title.

- Make a *Welcome Booklet* to give out to your children before they start in your class. Include photos of members of your team, your classroom, play areas and other areas in the school they will visit as well as information about life in your classroom.

- Welcome your children into the class every day with a big smile.

- A *Daily Messages* book is very useful (see also page 27).

A child-friendly classroom

A child-friendly classroom is a classroom where children have a sense of ownership and a good understanding of how it works. The classroom needs to be a place filled with fun, but it should also be safe and everything should be easily accessible. That way, it will be easy to manage.

This is achieved through planning and organisation. **Everything** should be labelled clearly and explained to adults and children, so everyone knows where to find things and also where to put them away!

Approach

This classroom is set up so that children and teachers can move around safely and with ease. It is bright and colourful and all aspects are organised and clearly defined.

To achieve this include:

1   A book corner, a maths corner and a literacy corner (see pages 10, 12, 14).

2   Table labels which identify where children should sit or carry out an activity (see page 17).

3   Clearly labelled pegs and trays for children.

4   Other defined areas such as an art area, an ICT area and a construction area (see page 9).

5   Clearly labelled trays that identify where things belong, for example a paper tray, a finished-work tray, a work-in-progress tray.

6   A giant timetable so that children can track their day and know what they are doing hour by hour, minute by minute! (See page 42).

7   It is important to tailor your classroom according to the age and ability of the children. For example, a noticeboard for upper juniors encourages independence and increased ownership of the classroom. However, for younger children who cannot read independently, this would be irrelevant.

8   In the same way, a giant clown on the wall by the classroom door is inappropriate for Year 6; but it is a fantastic way to show young children where to line up, as the head of the line must hold Clumsy Clown's hand!

Be a star! Keep the cloakroom tidy.

Peg and tray labels

- Always ensure a clear font is used and that labels are bright and cheerful.

- **Younger children:** include a picture that matches the initial of their name.

- A child's photo makes their peg ultra-accessible for them.

- **Older children:** a joined handwriting font makes peg labels more mature.

- Use a school or class logo as the basis of your peg label.

- Peg and tray labels could include the colours of house teams.

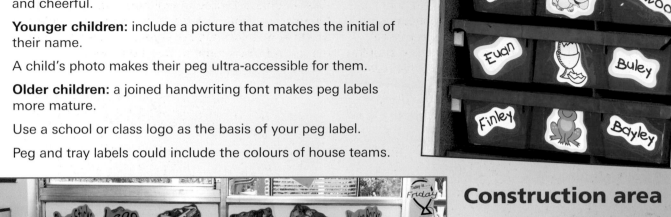

Construction area

- Provide a space for construction boxes in a designated construction area.

- Label each box clearly, identifying with a picture of what belongs inside.

Key Stage 2 noticeboard

- Back a board using school or class colours if possible.

- Make a clear title, *Our Class Noticeboard*, or you could be more quirky and give it a catchy title such as: *Notice the Notices!*

- Put notices on the board; but remember to update regularly! Older children could share in this responsibility.

Clumsy clown

- Paint a large, jolly clown with the class to ensure ownership.

- Cut out and tacky back onto the wall by the class door.

- Add brightly coloured, labelled balloons as an extra colour prompt.

Your book corner

Your book corner is a part of the classroom that specifically celebrates books and encourages reading. Children should be able to find all kinds of different books there: story books, picture books, fiction, non-fiction, topic-related books, poetry books and perhaps any school reading scheme. It should be a place where children can sit and read books individually, with a friend, or even in a small group. It's important that it is a stimulating place to be.

Approach

1 **Give your book corner a theme:** first and foremost, your book corner needs a theme to promote reading and draw attention to the space. It could be based on a topic you are studying, celebrate a particular author, or simply be designed to inspire children to read.

   You could include:

   - **Tasty texts:** created to link with a topic on food.

   - **Author-focused display:** for example, celebrate the author and illustrator partnership of Janet and Alan Ahlberg with laminated book covers and a selection of their books. This display also includes questions and key words relating to parts of a book.

   - **Fairy tales:** illustrates a genre the children are learning about. This display includes images and questions about fairy tales the children might know.

   - **Dive into a good book:** a display with a catchy title which features a giant diver and a range of covers of favourite books.

2 **Organise the books:** this is paramount if your book corner is to be an inviting place. The first step is to sort through your books so that only attractive, appealing books remain.

3 **Make the book corner user-friendly:** *Younger children:* arrange all picture books in easily accessible, labelled book boxes. Make sure that fiction or non-fiction books relate to a topic and are displayed separately, so children know where to find them. *Older children:* books could be arranged in boxes according to genre, e.g. fantasy books, adventure stories, sports stories, classic authors etc. This helps children to think about the kind of books they are choosing to read. An 'I'm not sure box' is useful. Children can put a finished book in this box if they are not sure where it belongs. Together the class put the books away.

4 **Reading tips:** display on laminated book shapes helpful hints for choosing a good book such as: *Read the blurb to see if you'll enjoy a book*. You can also include a *Teacher's top tips* section with ten of the teacher's favourite books, but don't forget to change them frequently!

1. Listen to recommendations from friends, teachers and family.

2. Learn about good books by reading book reviews and articles.

6. Look at the length of the book and the size of the print.

7. Read a few pages to see if it interests you.

Further ideas

- **Jump into a jungle of books:** paint animals, colour-mix leaves, create a jungle scene and hide book titles amongst the leaves. You could give the animals speech bubbles such as, 'What is your favourite book?'

- **Snap up a good book:** paint and collage large crocodile heads. Put in between their teeth words such as 'Books are exciting! Fun! Interesting!'

- **Pedal your way through a paperback:** paint, cut out and attach a bicycle to the wall. On the spokes put words relating to different genres.

- **Burrow into a good book:** paint a giant bookworm and put lots of books around it. Children should draw front covers of their favourite books and stick them around the bookworm.

- **Scoop up a good book:** collage a large digger. Create a building site scene using bricks that children could colour mix. Write on the bricks questions relating to books or book titles.

- **Hook up a rollicking read:** children can collage a big picture of Captain Hook with a huge hook. Dangling from his hook could be a selection of book titles.

Your maths corner

Every classroom needs a maths corner to house maths resources in an accessible, inviting way. It should celebrate maths and encourage children to think mathematically.

Approach

If possible, put your maths corner somewhere near a display board. In this maths corner, we have created a giant hundred square. This is a permanent display to help children with their maths work and it can also be used by the teacher when teaching maths strategies.

1 Create a two-coloured chequer board. We have chosen to back the board in green, and cut out and staple on yellow squares. Make a set of numbers 1 to 100 and back on orange. Once the board is complete, tacky back to prevent it getting tatty. Add a title and questions to encourage children to use the hundred square in different ways.

2 You are creating a resource area, so label trays of small items of maths equipment, e.g. calculators, clocks, money, number lines etc.

3 Larger equipment, or items that are used regularly such as cubes, 2D and 3D shapes, counters, giant clock, giant egg timers, maths books and rulers etc. should be put in attractive, inviting baskets on easily accessible surfaces.

4 Display on the wall, resources and teaching prompts appropriate to the age range and ability of the children. Here, the class teacher has provided aids for counting in twos on bicycles (to link with two wheels!) and time-related words are displayed on clocks.

5 Shape prompts, key words and numbers should be displayed all over the maths area. Everything should be bright and colourful, and if you feel daring add a few dots or stars in the spaces to add further interest!

Penguin Small's nippy number bonds

Where possible, create a maths display near your maths corner. This should be linked to a topic that is going to be taught to the children. Once the term has begun, change the focus of the display to include children's work.

1   Back the board in blue and cut an icicle border out of white paper.

2   Create a catchy title. Cut out letters using a template in light blue, back onto deep blue and then silver.

3   Make icebergs using white paper and grey chalk to give an iceberg effect.

4   Chalk pastel some penguins in very cute shapes. If you are not great at drawing use a clip art penguin and enlarge to A3. Place the penguins in various positions on the icebergs.

5   Cut out circles and stick on photocopied numbers. Use the circles to give a snowy effect on the picture. The numbers on the circles should all relate to the theme of number bonds.

6   Make large, clear questions for the children to answer relating to the display. Back on a new colour so that they stand out. Yellow was chosen to match the penguins' yellow beaks. Place the questions around the edge of the display.

Further ideas

- A giant multiplication square (see page 50).
- Vocabulary relating to the four functions, addition, subtraction, division, multiplication.
- A giant clock with time-related words.
- A place-value board.
- A board focusing on units of measure or converting measures.

Your literacy corner

Every classroom needs an area dedicated to literacy. This should house all your literacy resources so that they are accessible to the children, but it also should be an area that celebrates literacy and promotes the children's interest in language.

Approach

Key Stage 1 literacy area

Create an area specifically for all your literacy resources to encourage thinking about literacy and support children's learning, through a range of visual aids and prompts.

Firefighter display

1   Back the board in a strong colour, create a border using red paper and add contrasting dots.

2   Paint and collage a large firefighter with a hose.

3   Create a title called *Fight the Fires*.

4   Cut out pale-blue water drops and add phonemes on to them in a deeper shade of blue.

5   Make flame/fire shapes and add pictures related to the phonemes.

6   Add questions to encourage the children to match the phonemes to the pictures.

7   You are creating a resource area, so label trays that relate to literacy equipment, e.g. word finders, guidelines, spelling resources etc.

8   Place equipment used regularly (e.g. pencils, pens, magnetic letters, exercise books etc.) on any available surfaces in baskets or boxes that are visually attractive.

9   You could use any available wall space in your literacy area to display further resources and teaching prompts to aid children in their literacy work. These should be appropriate to the age range and ability of the children.

Key Stage 2 literacy area

VCOP display

1. Back the board in a pale colour. Cut out and add a red border with contrasting dots.

2. Paint a large police officer and place in the centre of the board. Make a set of extra-large VCOP letters and the words: vocabulary, connectives, openers and punctuation. Display on the board next to the police officer.

3. Include questions to stimulate children's thinking about the VCOP concept.

4. As for the Key Stage 1 area, include labelled trays, learning aids, prompts and resources displayed attractively. Make sure they are relevant to the age and ability of the children: for example, age appropriate connectives, punctuation prompts (see page 48), spellings of the week, upper and lower case letters, a list of different genres etc. Don't forget to change the displays frequently to stimulate children's interest. All these resources should be large and backed on bright colours so they look interesting and fun!

Further ideas

- Create a display to highlight different text types and their features. This could be a giant chef who 'Cooks up a good story/poem/recount/letter/diary' etc. Bubbling inside large cooking pots for each text type are their identifying features.

- Create a word wall which includes key words for the term that children can access when writing.

- Celebrate children's use of powerful vocabulary by collecting words they have used successfully in their writing on a 'WOW!' words display.

Managing your Classroom

Grouping your children

Within your classroom, everything should function in a structured, clear way. Effective grouping helps not only to maximise children's learning, but can also create a positive and purposeful environment where they can work and play.

There are several ways that you can group your children and each has its own benefits. The groups could be changed every term, or every half term.

Ability grouping

This allows you to differentiate and provide work that caters for learners of different abilities ensuring maximum learning takes place. Depending on age and ability, you may need different groupings for different subjects.

Mixed-ability grouping

This allows children of varying ability to share their knowledge. It can extend more able children, through developing their explanation skills, while allowing the less able to learn from their peers. With experience, a teacher can judge if a group is working and will move children around so they get maximum benefit.

Friendship groups

Children are put into groups with children that they might not normally socialise with. This type of grouping allows children to develop their social skills and can have a positive effect on behaviour within the class.

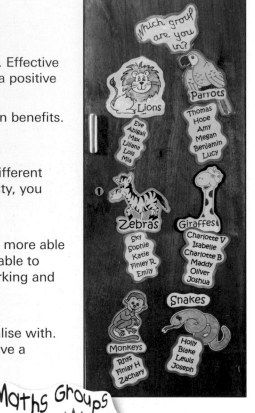

Approach

Our groups

1   Back the board in blue (or any colour with special associations for the children). Make a title using a chosen font from the computer. Choose colours that complement the backing.

2   Give each group an appropriate name (we chose names that are related to the topic that the children are learning about). Source attractive pictures and back them on different colours.

3   Take head shots of the children, cut out and back on red. Place the head shots around a group picture.

4   In order to make this board effective, ensure that it is big enough so children can see clearly which group they are in! Children's names could be added to the display.

Further ideas

Table labels: if you want children to sit at specific tables at a particular time, for example, at the beginning of the day, make large labels with the same named pictures as the different groups. Tacky back these on the children's tables. This is a really effective way to make sure the children know where they should sit.

Work folders: make labels that match the groups and tacky back onto folders or giant, zipped wallets. You can then use these to put children's work into each day. Each group has a different folder, so that both you and the children can find the work easily.

Flashcards: a useful strategy when working with younger children is to have a set of flashcards at your fingertips, so that when you are sending groups off the carpet, e.g. to line up, to get ready for lunch, or to play a game, you can show them the flashcard as well as saying the group name. Each flashcard has a picture of a different group. This provides a visual cue for the children which they find really useful.

Rules and rewards

At the start of the school year, it is important to establish a rules and rewards system within your class that will make it a good place to be. This should involve all kinds of behaviour, such as trying hard, listening well, sharing etc. Always make sure that your rules are visible and clearly explained. This is your classroom behaviour code, and if it is too complicated and too wordy it will not be effective. Your reward system should also be simple and easy to understand. Often a visual reward for younger children is more effective than awarding house points, which is a better strategy for older children.

Here are some ways to display classroom rules:

Approach

Totem pole

As a class, create a set of rules. Divide the class into groups and give each a round, cardboard disc. Using kitchen roll and glue, each group creates and paints an image to symbolise a class rule: for example, a pair of touching hands for being kind. Attach the discs to a large totem-pole tube and add feathers and decorations to create a vibrant effect. Place the totem pole in the corner of the classroom where everyone can see it.

Whale award acrostic

Choose a class symbol that can be used to display your class rules visually. Here, the letters of the word 'whale' spell out the class rules. Once again, display in the classroom where all children can see.

To create this display: cut out the letters 'Whale Award'. Using the initial letter from the word 'Whale', write a sentence or phrase to highlight each of the class rules: W = Work together, H = Help each other, A = Always be kind etc. Back on blue and display as an acrostic. Include pictures of whales around the edge of the display.

Busy bee display

Use the school emblem or class name to help create rules and display them. Our school emblem is a bumble bee and our Year 1 class uses this to help remember their class rules. Each day they are busy **bee**-ing kind, busy **bee**-ing a hard worker, busy **bee**-ing cooperative etc.

Reward systems

Key Stage 1

Badges: it is vital for younger children that the reward system is explicitly linked to class rules. It is also important for any reward to be big and visible, and that there is a home-school link, so that parents can reward children at home as well. A child's positive behaviour is celebrated by being awarded a badge, which they can wear home for the evening and bring back to school the next day. Badges should have an image identical to the one on the class rules and a specific class rule on the back, e.g. 'I have been busy bee-ing kind!' You could even make silver and gold badges for really special occasions!

Key Stage 2

Older children enjoy the challenge of winning house or team points and they can join a team at the start of their time in Key Stage 2. In each class, display who is in which team by putting photos of children on a display board next to the team they belong to. At the end of each week, it is good practice to collect all the points and celebrate the winning team with a cup or a reward, for example, an extra five minutes playtime.

Further ideas

Class of the week cup: this is awarded in assembly to the class who carries out their rules the best, everybody cheers and celebrates their success.

Lunch-time laws: it is good practice to have a set of lunchtime rules clearly visible in the classroom.

Nellie rules: one class used the idea that an elephant never forgets. As a class they decided on their rules and took photos of children carrying them out. For example, Nellie the elephant never forgets to share, so they took a photo of two children working together.

Targets

Target-setting helps give children ownership of their learning. In many schools, teachers are encouraged to set children targets that they can work towards throughout the half-term or term. It is vital that:

T argets are set regularly
A chieveable
R elevant and meaningful
G oals to work towards
E everyone makes progress
T ime to test your knowledge
S uccess is rewarded

Schools usually have different systems for different age groups. In Key Stage 1, it may be more appropriate to set group targets. These should be on display, referred to regularly, and there should be no more than one target for literacy or numeracy. In Key Stage 2, targets are tailored to the individual child. Children should have targets for maths and literacy and depending on their age and ability, either one or two targets. As a school we would never set more than two targets. For example, a child's literacy target might be to remember to use a range of connectives: 'and', 'because', 'so', in their own writing. A maths target might be to learn number bonds up to 10. The most effective way to set targets is to have a clear and consistent approach running throughout the school.

- Targets should be the result of the teacher's assessment of independent maths and literacy work. For example, a piece of unaided writing and a test covering different areas of the maths curriculum.

- From this assessment, the teacher and the child work together to decide on something they need to improve.

- Children should write their target on an illustrated literacy or numeracy target card.

- The cards are then kept in an accessible place for children, either in individual trays, or in a pre-made pocket in their literacy and numeracy books.

- Children should demonstrate to the teacher that they can consistently work towards a learning target. It is important that children show this more than once. You might use stamps or stickers on the target card to show every time they achieve a target.

- Some schools introduce a 'prove it' session, where children have the opportunity to demonstrate that they have achieved a target.

- Once a target has been achieved, it is important that this is recognised and a new target is set. One idea would be to send a postcard home to the child's parents, congratulating a child on achieving a target and highlighting their **new** target. This process makes both child and their parent aware of what needs to be done to improve even further. Another idea is to reward the child with a prize which he or she can choose from a box of assorted treats or prizes.

Approach

Terrific targets

In this display, the word 'target' becomes an acrostic making the target system meaningful to children.

1   Back the board and add a border decorated with gold stars.

2   Create a title, 'Terrific Targets', using a computer font and the three colours of your display: red, blue and gold.

3   Cut out the word 'target' from red paper backed on gold paper and put each letter on a target shape.

4   Write the acrostic sentences on the computer. Print out and back on red paper.

6   At the start of the year, photograph each child in a celebration pose. Laminate and pop in a bag by the target board. If a child achieves their target, they can place their photo on the board.

Reach for the stars

This display could be used in a reception or Key Stage 1 classroom. Always display your target board in a central place, so that it can be referred to regularly when teaching.

1   Make a title using a template and cutting out the letters from dark blue paper. Back as a whole word on silver.

2   Create the word STARS using silver letters backed on blue star shapes.

3   Make giant stars from silver paper backed on blue.

4   Label each star with the name of a group.

5   Make laminated literacy targets on giant pencils and numeracy targets on abacuses.

6   Make captions with questions and phrases about the target and place around the display.

7   Cut out lots of silver and blue stars and place all around the display.

Further ideas

Other themes or titles for target boards could be: (football) Tackle your Targets, Our Goals, (Racing track) Race to the Finishing line, (Archery) Aim for your Targets etc.

Helping in the classroom

Children love to help in the classroom. As a teacher, it's up to you to create an environment in which they can help and have ownership of the way their classroom works. Simple jobs such as snack monitor, lunchtime monitor, register monitor etc, are tasks that children can be responsible for and they will help keep your classroom neat, tidy and in excellent working order. Create enough jobs for at least half the class and make sure that these jobs are rotated weekly. This will keep children interested and give them a sense of responsibility. Often, having two children for each job ensures that it gets done quickly and thoroughly. Here are some possible jobs to include on your job board.

- **Chair monitor:** pushes the chairs in throughout the day and pops them up on the table at the end of the day.

- **Snack monitor:** gives out the snacks to children.

- **Lunch box monitor:** places lunchboxes on the tables ready for lunch.

- **Head of the line monitor:** this avoids conflict amongst children.

- **Tail of the line monitor:** checks we all get to the correct place.

- **Pencil monitor:** checks pencils are sharpened and tidied away.

- **Book/library monitor:** checks books are put away.

- **Coat monitor:** checks the coats are all on the appropriate pegs.

- **Register/message monitor:** takes messages to the school office.

- **Playtime monitor:** puts games and activities out in the playground and helps tidy away at the end of the day.

- **Litter monitor:** collects the litter during playtime and snack time using a litter picker provided by the teacher.

- **Washing up monitor:** washes up cups and paint pots.

- **Compost monitor:** collects and empties the compost bins each day.

Approach

Helping is fun!

1   Create a chequered background.

2   Make a snappy title, for example *Helper Heroes, Helping Hands* etc.

3   Using clip art, find pictures to represent the jobs. For example, for a pencil monitor, use a pencil. Laminate and put on the board.

4   Print out and laminate each child's name. Place the names in a bag. When selecting monitors, pull out a name at a time and let each child choose his or her own job.

Caterpillar display

In school, space is often an issue. A board may not be available. This display fills a space that was not very attractive and means the teacher has a Helpers board close to where she teaches.

1   Make a caterpillar using different shades of green. (Use the head and tail for your head and tail of line jobs.)

2   Once again, print out a collection of pictures to represent jobs, back on yellow and place on different sections of the caterpillar.

3   Use laminated photos of children to indicate what job they have chosen that week.

Further ideas

- To make a job more exciting and appealing, provide a good gimmick. A badge or bib to wear, or special piece of equipment is always a winner!

- Another way to create a Helpers board would be to replace the clip art with photos of children doing the job. Instead of an image of a pencil, you could have a photo of a child tidying the pencil pots.

Systems for storage

Storage and clutter is always an issue in schools and classrooms. It is vital to create storage systems so that you and the children can access equipment and resources quickly and easily. Within your classroom, it is important to create specific areas for children's resources such as construction toys, small world toys, books, pens, and pencils etc, and for teacher resources, like topic boxes, role-play resources etc. Creating places for things to belong means that, in your classroom, they don't get lost and clutter does not collect!

Approach

Storage shelves

This space has been created in a reception classroom to house a mixture of topic and role-play resources.

1   Construct a simple but sturdy shelving unit.

2   Collect boxes in bright, inviting colours.

3   Organise the boxes so that resources fit in each box.

4   Label each box clearly using a contrasting colour. When making the labels, ensure a clear font is used and the labels are large and very visible. Tacky back onto the boxes.

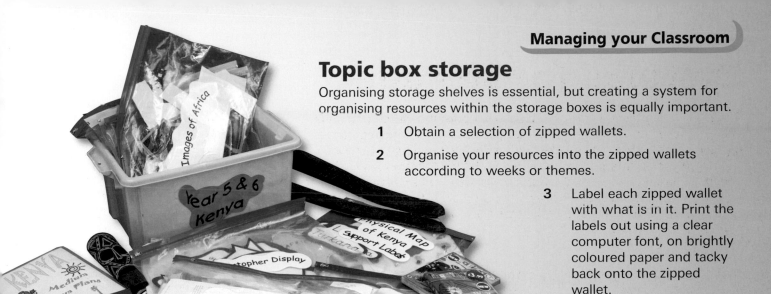

Topic box storage

Organising storage shelves is essential, but creating a system for organising resources within the storage boxes is equally important.

1   Obtain a selection of zipped wallets.

2   Organise your resources into the zipped wallets according to weeks or themes.

3   Label each zipped wallet with what is in it. Print the labels out using a clear computer font, on brightly coloured paper and tacky back onto the zipped wallet.

4   Always check resources after using them. Remake anything tatty before putting it away. It is such a nice surprise when you revisit the boxes to find resources beautifully made and all ready to go!

Children's storage

Organising children's resources is as important as organising yourself. If areas are accessible to children, they can tidy things away, and if everything has a designated place, then the classroom is inviting and clutter-free.

This storage space is for construction toys and play equipment, and is for both children and adults to access.

- Consider the resources you have and obtain appropriate boxes and bins, e.g. bins for mats, large and small boxes for smaller items.

- Label boxes clearly.

- Create a title for the area, such as 'Construction Corner'. You could make this out of cogs, bricks, diggers to relate to the construction theme.

Further ideas

Making the most of every available space in the classroom is a must. See how, by finding the right-sized boxes, shelves on the back of a bookcase can store small toys and play equipment.

Organising yourself

The key ingredient to an organised classroom is YOU! Being organised is an essential part of being an excellent teacher and coping with everyday school life which can, on occasions, be hectic!

What does it mean?

Organise your own space

In most classrooms, the teacher has a cupboard. This is an area that often becomes a dumping ground for things that you are not sure what to do with. Use your cupboard effectively and it can really help you to stay on top of things.

- Use boxes that are labelled. For example: an autumn, spring and summer box creates an easy-to-manage system to store the term's resources.

- A things-to-do tray is for items that need immediate attention.

- A tray for stationery such as scissors, sellotape, etc means you have them at your fingertips.

- Allocate a box to your teaching assistant so s/he has a place to put materials.

- Keep resources that you use less frequently on the top shelf (e.g. Christmas resources).

- Put notices on the cupboard door that are essential for making your day/week run smoothly, e.g. a class timetable, a parent-helper rota, medical notes about children, staff meeting dates, children's groups, relevant timetables etc.

Further ideas

Organise your planning

All teachers have to plan. This is done on the computer but keeping a paper copy is a good habit to adopt. Make a planning book with detachable sheets. Some teachers produce a separate literacy and numeracy book; others produce a general planning book. It can include a timetable for each week and a good tip is to leave a blank page for things to do or notes to help you each week.

Organising your classroom assistants

Maximising your teaching assistant's effectiveness is all about organisation and communication. Teachers often face the problem that they do not have time to talk through all the things they want to achieve in a day with their teaching assistant. Therefore, a *Jobs to do* book is a good system to adopt. Write down anything that you'd like your teaching assistant to do whenever he or she has a spare five minutes. This could range from sticking homework in books to spending time with a child giving extra support with letter formation. Write things down, and you won't have to remember absolutely everything at the beginning of every day.

Organising your day

- This is vital. Always ensure that you are ready to start the day by the time children arrive. There is nothing worse than running around like a headless chicken first thing in the morning.

- Always greet the children and parents with a BIG SMILE!

- Have a *Daily Messages* book in your hand to write down messages from parents and children as they talk to you. Throughout the day, anyone in your team can add extra messages for you to give to parents, e.g. if a child has felt sick. At the end of the day, refer to the book to remind children of things they need to know, e.g. who is picking them up if different from usual.

- Create a *Today's resources* box so everything you need for the day is at your fingertips.

- Make a large *Today's activity* board that you can write on and wipe off every day.

- Make record-keeping books central and accessible to everyone: e.g. reading record books, observation record book, or art records. Some schools keep daily records on computer and add to them with hand-held devices like mobiles, so that individual observations can be uploaded at the end of the day.

Display in your Classroom

Types of display

If you want your classroom to be colourful, vibrant and stimulating, you need to think up and create a constantly changing selection of high-quality displays. It is important that they are varied and for different purposes. Effective displays are a powerful tool for learning and should never be seen as a wallpaper exercise.

There are many different types of displays you can make, all of which have a particular purpose.

Celebrating children's achievement

At the end of a project, topic or unit of work it is vital to use display in your classroom to celebrate children's work and their success. A display like this also serves as a constant visual reinforcement of their learning.

The wonderful world of chocolate

The display above shows a range of art, literacy and design technology work that the children produced as part of a cross-curricular project on food. Notice the influence of Roald Dahl's *Charlie and the Chocolate Factory*!

Handa's Surprise

This display was produced following a literacy unit of work on the story *Handa's Surprise*. The children's story work is displayed together with key words from the story and the children's artwork.

Interactive displays

Interactive displays encourage children to engage with resources to develop their learning.

Frog's world

This display allows children to experience the life cycle of a frog first-hand, as a real pond is created in the classroom. The teacher used the class water tray which is filled with frogspawn, pond water and plants. The excitement is quite magical as children check the pond daily for changes, watching the frogspawn hatch into tadpoles which begin growing into frogs. The display is used for group work and children use magnifying glasses and collecting pots to examine the contents of the pond. Questions are displayed around the pond and the display behind it of the life cycle of a frog provides information for the children, showing them what to look for, and reinforcing their learning. A safety notice could also be added for the children and creatures: Be gentle! We're all alive in here!

Information displays

Information displays teach children facts about a topic or subject they are learning about.

Journey of a letter

This display was put up at the beginning of a reception class topic on letter writing. It provides information about the journey of a letter from writing and posting a letter to receiving it. This display is used by the teacher as a teaching tool before the children draw their own flow chart of the journey of a letter. The children then write letters, walk to the post office and post them. Photos are added to the display, to show children taking part in the journey of their letter.

Funnybones science

This is another information display put up at the beginning of a science unit on bones. It uses key words and questions together with a skeleton to aid the children's learning and can be used as a teaching tool. Again, children's science work will be added as the unit of work progresses.

Functional displays

These displays help your classroom to function and can remain in place all year round.

Sports clubs and timetable

This gives children information about lunchtime and after-school clubs. It includes photos of children enjoying different clubs, together with a timetable so that children can plan which ones they want to attend.

Master bedroom
Larder
Day Nursery
Parlour
Kitchen
Dining Room
We worked in groups to design and make our own Victorian room. Can you guess which room we made?
Drawing Room
Guest room
Scullery
Night Nursery
Servant's Bedroom

Upstairs Downstairs

What was the scullery used for?
How were Victorian houses heated?
What was a chamber pot used for?
In which room would you find a 'range' and some flagstones?
How many servants were used in a rich Victorian house?
What sort of room was the parlour?
What did a housekeeper do?
What was used instead of a washing machine?
Were all Victorian houses the same?
How much did a maid get paid for working in a large house?

Subject-specific displays

These displays focus on specific subjects such as history or design technology.

This is an original way to display children's design and technology work as part of a project on the Victorians. The children were asked to work in groups to design and make a room in a Victorian house. The finished pieces have been put together to make a complete house, to give the children the opportunity to appreciate their own and others' work. This is displayed together with designs and photos of the individual teams which have constructed each room.

As primary school teachers we are passionate about displays. To us, display should be:

D isplaying quality work
I nteractive and inspirational
S timulating and vibrant
P urposeful
L ively and engaging
A ttractive and colourful
Y ield success

31

Creating

An essential element of an excellent display is the choice of lettering which helps to pull everything together. Some schools have ready-made templates and use the same lettering for every display, but with computers and photocopiers, lettering can be so much more creative.

When creating lettering it is important to think about:

- **Size:** always make your lettering large. No lettering should be smaller than A4 and the ideal size is A3. Obviously, the size of the board will determine the size of each letter, but it is essential that lettering is as clear and visual as possible.

- **Colour:** choice of colour will often depend on your display theme and the most effective lettering will probably include colours used in the display.

- **Style:** being creative with your lettering can and will enhance your displays. Where possible, try and style lettering to suit the theme of the display. For example, a display on winter could have lettering in blue and white with the white paper being used to create an icicle or snow effect on each letter which could then be backed on silver.

- **Positioning:** you can put lettering almost anywhere on your display – in the centre, to the side, at the top or bottom of the board. It can be straight or wobbly, flat or bowed.

- **Reusable:** always make your lettering to a high standard and laminate it so that it can be reused if necessary.

Lettering ideas

Mad about milk: this lettering was created using the font Flubber. The template was made A4 size and cut out in white. The white letters were then backed in pink and black cow patches were added to create the 'cow' effect. The colour choice was intended to make the children think of cows.

Handa's Surprise: this lettering was created from the front cover of the actual book. The lettering was enlarged onto white A3 paper. The letters were cut out and backed on the appropriate colours, and coloured using pencil crayons to match the backing.

P-P-P-Penguins: this lettering was created using an image from the display and then the lettering was placed on top of the cut-out image. This image was created from clip art, but it could have been children's own drawings, or drawings created in class, enlarged on the photocopier and backed on an appropriate colour. The lettering was cut out of a standard school template.

Funny Bones: this lettering was made from a computer font called Bones. Each letter was printed out on A4 paper, cut out and backed on yellow paper.

Shapes: this lettering was created by cutting out large black shapes and placing shiny cut-out letters on top. The lettering was created from a standard school font but enlarged to A4. The black shapes were A3 size.

33

Backgrounds and borders

Creating a dynamic display often begins with the choice of background. This can range from one main colour, to a chequered board, to a themed background, to setting a scene using a different material or fabric. The most important thing is to choose a background that links in with the theme of the display.

Background display ideas

- **One colour:** the colour chosen can link to the theme, e.g. a Greek display could have an orange background with a black border, or a sunflower display may have a pale blue background to show the sky.

- **Chequered board:** this can be created by backing the board in one colour, cutting out squares (25 mm is a good size) from the second colour and creating a chequer effect. This type of background can be used to add energy to the display, or perhaps the theme suggests it. Two shades of blue could be used for a water display, or black-and-white checks for a Victorian display. A pizza display could have a chequered red-and-white background as a 'table cloth'.

- **Themed board:** this is a background that links directly with the subject. An African animal display could have a stripy background to echo a zebra's black and white stripes.

- **Setting the scene:** this can be striking, but the work that accompanies the display must be large and backed in a contrasting colour, so that it does not get lost in the background. For example, an Egyptian display could set the scene with sand dunes, palm trees and pyramids.

- **A variety of different materials or fabrics:** this is often a clever stimulus for a background to a display. A World War II display could have a camouflage-netting background, or a display that focuses on the seaside could have a background created from hessian material, yellow to depict the sand and blue for the sea.

- **Borders:** the choice of a border for a display is optional, but can bring a display into focus. Once again, the choice of border should link into the actual display. For example, the William Morris display includes a border created out of photocopied examples of his work. The border links in with the title and brings the whole display together.

Border display ideas

Borders can be created in lots of ways. They don't have to be wiggly. They could be:

- Straight
- Zigzag
- Curved
- Icicles
- Cave border

- Lined
- Spotty
- Squared/Castle edge
- Island or land border
- Objects: for example, handprints, leaves, cogs etc.

However, a border is not vital to every display. It is nice to have some displays in your classroom that do not have a border at all.

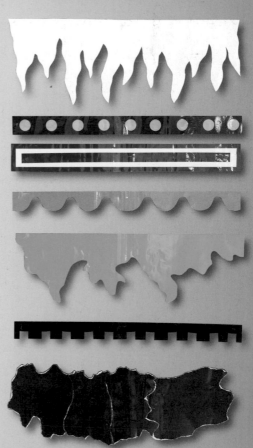

Labels and captions

Labels and captions provide an important part of a display. They serve three important purposes:

- They can provide an explanation of the display.

- They provide keywords, phrases or questions for the children to read to consolidate their learning.

- They fit in between the children's work and 'lift' the display to make it visually arresting.

Approach

Labels and captions can take various forms.

- **Keywords**
  In this display (right), keywords have been used to label the giant ladybird to consolidate the children's learning about the parts of a ladybird. These have been created using a computer font and printed out in A3 so they are clearly legible. Children's work will also be added to the display.

- **Phrases**
  As part of their work on butterflies, the children created an acrostic about butterflies. The teacher asked different children to write phrases which were displayed alongside their artwork. Again, these have been written large so they are legible.

- **Questions and answers**
  The history display on the opposite page focuses on the development of the bicycle. It includes questions for the children to read and answer, stimulating their ideas and revising key facts they have learnt. It also includes a pictorial timeline, together with captions to explain this.

- **Using pictures or symbols**
  Children love puzzles to solve and if you include some of these on some of your displays, it gives them something to think about in any of those moments in which they 'drift off'! In this display the children are just beginning their topic on 'Britain since the 1930s'. As a stimulus, the teacher has displayed a range of black and white photographs relating to different decades and poses the question 'Can you match the photos to the correct decade?'

Further ideas

Functional signage around the classroom should be attractive as well as useful. Again, this can be produced using a computer font, or handwritten by the children and laminated. Pictures, clip art or symbols can be used to make signs more attractive and user-friendly, especially for younger children.

From start to finish

Here we describe how to assemble a display. It is helpful to get everything ready before you begin: colour scheme chosen, title made, work backed, and captions created. In this way, you can be sure there is enough useful, quality work to fill the display board as you want.

Pedal power

This reception display was inspired by *The Jolly Postman*. The children had a visit from the Jolly Postman and his bicycle. They learnt about the parts of his bicycle and how it moves when they are pushed or pulled. The children sketched and labelled his bicycle and made a bicycle using weaving and collage. They made giant bicycles out of different materials and they also drew a bicycle on the computer using an art package.

Creating the display

1   **Backing the board:** green was chosen in contrast to the yellow, red and blue used for the backing and the title. Always hang your paper in the same direction, either landscape or portrait.

2   **Focal point:** make a bicycle from everyday materials. Using a glue gun, glue two large hoops onto the display to represent bicycle wheels. Use cardboard tubes for the frame, draw in the pedals and handlebars, use pencils for the spokes and a rubber spot for the seat.

3   **Title:** create the title using two of the three main display colours. Cut the letters out of a computer-generated font and place on large blue or red circles. Arrange the title at various angles. You could overlap each circle slightly, if you liked.

4 **Design:** staple children's large, collaged bicycles all over the board. It is usually best to put the largest pieces of work in position first! Add the sketched bicycles and photographs, followed by the ICT bicycles. Check that the work is distributed across the display in a balanced fashion. Some work could be bowed to create a 3D effect.

5 **Captions and signs:** create captions with a computer font, cut out and back on red, blue and yellow before adding to the display, filling any gaps. Again, you can bow the labels to create a 3D effect. Take care that the signs and captions are close to the work they refer to. 'We made collage bicycles' should be next to a collaged bicycle.

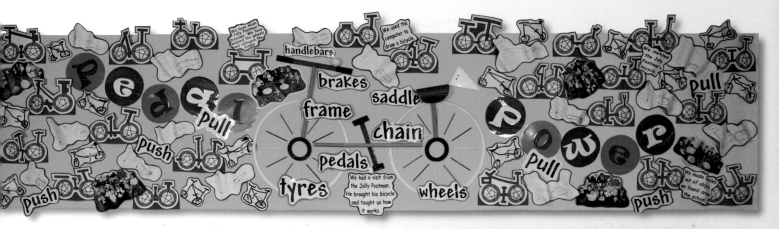

6 **Spots:** spots can liven up a display. They also bring colours together and fill any unwanted spaces!

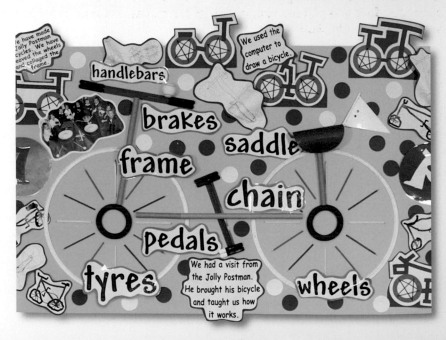

Wartime Blitz

This display was made with a Year 5 class as part of a cross-curricular topic, Britain since 1930s. It was initially put up to stimulate the children's interest and then used as a teaching tool to establish what the children already knew about World War II. During the project, children's own work was added to celebrate their achievement.

Approach

1. **Backing:** back the board using old newspaper or brown parcel paper to create a period effect.

2. **Border:** use camouflage netting to make a border around the display. This can be bought very cheaply from toy shops.

3. **Title:** create the title *Wartime Blitz* using pale green paper backed on darker green paper. Arrange the title in a zigzag. It is fine for the letters to overlap, as long as you can still read them! Bow the letters to create a 3D effect.

4. **Design:** here, the teacher has put up black and white wartime photographs to promote discussion and thinking. Arrange the photos on the board in groups. As a contrast to the title, arrange them straight and flat (2D) to the board. You could overlap them a little but be careful not to cover up any important details.

5. **Captions and labels:** as the main purpose of this display is to promote thinking and discussion, the teacher has added questions that relate to the photos. These are placed on the display in a zigzag effect and are bowed to look 3D, like the title.

6   **Children's work:** once children have finished their own
    work, arrange this on this display, (here the children have
    made wartime posters). To make sure that the children's
    work shows to good advantage, first, take everything off
    except the title. Then arrange everything, filling in any gaps
    afterwards with black and white photos and questions.

Finally take time to stand back and admire everyone's work!

When creating a display always remember…

lettering   colour choice

FOCAL POINT

QUALITY WORK   labels

back your
work   2D AND 3D EFFECTS

Resourcing your Classroom

General resources

Resourcing your classroom effectively is crucial to ensuring that your lessons are equipped for the appropriate learning. In this chapter we have outlined resources that we believe are paramount to a successful school day.

Daily timetable

This resource is vital especially for those children who need to know exactly what their day consists of in order to remain calm and not become anxious. A giant classroom timetable allows children to see what they are doing throughout the day.

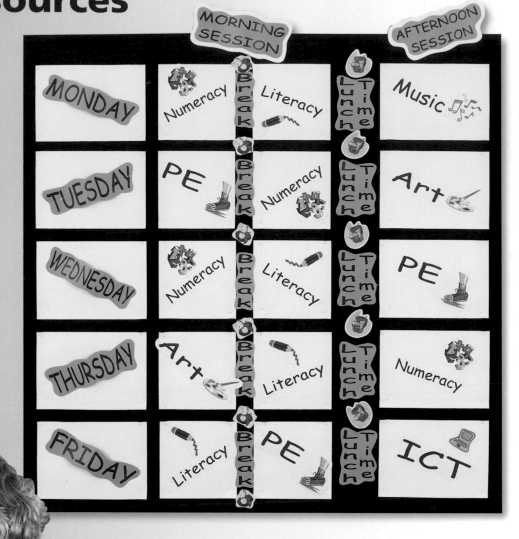

Approach

1 Make a timetable template using two different backing papers. Put the days of the week down the left side and the times of the school day across the top.

2 Identify playtime and lunchtime breaks and indicate in words and pictures what the children will be doing throughout the day. Display on the wall or a board in the classroom.

Small individual timetables can also be a great support resource for children who worry about the 'unknown'.

Exercise books

Most schools use exercise books for children's work. These tend to be used daily and therefore need to be tough as well as colourful. In the photos below we have shown a selection of Key Stage 1 and Key Stage 2 books. As you can see, the books have bright front covers created using a clip art picture that relates to the subject: a clown with numbers has been used for the numeracy book, whilst an ink pot and quill pen has been used for the literacy books. The red topic books are used for the children's cross-curricular work. These designs should vary from class to class. The children's names are on the front of all the books. Using a computer font create, print, cut and stick each child's name on the front of their books. All the books have been covered in plastic book covering or tacky back. This ensures they stay looking good for longer!

Pencil pots

This is a resource that all classrooms need but which can cause teachers a small headache. It is often difficult to buy inexpensive, but attractive pencil pots that are big enough for the classroom. Below we have shown how a simple empty tin can be transformed into a fun pencil pot holder.

Approach

1   Collect lots of clean, empty tin cans. Make sure there are no sharp edges on them.

2   Cover each can with bright paper and add a label or colourful dots or stars to make the pot more interesting.

3   Cover the cans in plastic covering or tacky back and arrange your pencils so they are facing the correct way up.

Pencil pots can be placed in the middle of each table but often they get knocked over and are generally in the way. Our experience tells us that best practice is to create a pencil pot area, so children can take pencils whenever they need them. Don't forget to make the area safe and convenient to access.

Finished and unfinished trays

Within a busy classroom we are always producing lots of fabulous work, but where do we put it? One of the most simple and useful systems in a classroom is a finished and unfinished tray. Two simple trays can be used to create a resource that will help you and your children to organise their work.

Everyday resources for creative teaching

Being a creative teacher and using resources that will stimulate and excite the children often involves thinking outside the box. Resources that are bright and attractive can instantly make a lesson lively and memorable. Below several resources are listed that we use daily within the classroom to enhance carpet sessions and make group activities more engaging.

- **Feely box:** this can be created out of a large box covered with coloured paper and made to look fun. Cut out a hole in the top big enough to fit your hand. Tacky back the box to ensure it stays attractive. A feely box during carpet sessions adds tension and suspense. A child puts their hand in to feel a 3D shape and describes it to the class, who tries to guess what it is, within a specified time limit. Then the child reveals the object to show if the class was correct.

- **Large egg timer:** these are brilliant when taking turns, for example, when sharing a computer with a friend. They can add a competitive aspect to the lesson, for example, you could ask: "How many ways of making 10 can you write in a minute?" The size of the egg timer is what makes it exciting and it is a resource that no class should be without.

- **Spinners:** these are manufactured from wood, painted in sections and varnished to keep them looking like new. Decide what you would like to use your spinner for. Create the appropriate labels, using a computer font or clip art, and tacky back onto each section of the spinner. To reuse them, simply peel off the labels and replace with new ones. They are a good resource for group activities, e.g. for playing money games where your spinner could have a different coin marked on each section.

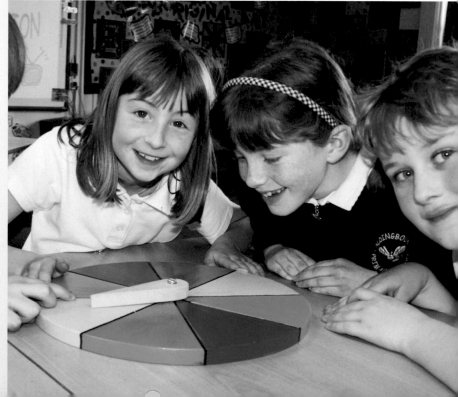

- **Spots:** these can be made out of thick card. Cut out large circles, paint and laminate to ensure that they are durable. Tacky back on numbers, words and pictures as required. Spots can be used both for carpet session activities and a great many group games. To play *Cross the River*, place the spots in a line like stepping stones over the river. Each spot has a picture of an object on the front and the word on the back. Children have to predict the initial letter of the word. To see if they are correct, they turn over the 'stepping stone'. If they are right, they can progress to the next one. Who can get furthest across the river?

  They can also be used to organise children by, for example, giving each child a spot to sit or stand on. You can also use thick plastic place mats cut to shape. Make sure they aren't slippy on the carpet.

- **Bottle:** a beautiful coloured bottle is a great resource to have in your classroom. This can be used as a resource for selecting children fairly. Place the children in a circle, spin the bottle and whoever it points towards has to answer the question or carry out a task.

- **Jingle ball:** a large, brightly-coloured ball that makes a jingle sound can add excitement to a carpet session or group activity. For example, a class could retell a story using a jingle ball. One child begins the story and then passes the jingle ball across the circle for a friend to continue, and so on.

Literacy resources

Earlier in this book, we talked about the importance of having a literacy corner in your classroom to house all your literacy resources. In this section, we would like to look at the sort of resources that you might find in and around this area, and how the children use them to aid their learning.

Phonics frieze

In any infant or lower junior classroom, it is essential to have some kind of phonics or alphabet frieze to support your phonics work in the classroom. This should be matched to whichever phonics scheme your school follows, and should be displayed prominently, ensuring that every letter is clearly visible for the children. The teacher should constantly make use of the phonics frieze while teaching, and encourage the children to use it when reading and writing.

Flashcards to match the frieze are also an invaluable resource. These should be kept where the teacher can access them easily, as they should be used at regular intervals throughout the day to reinforce the children's phonic knowledge.

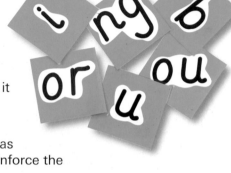

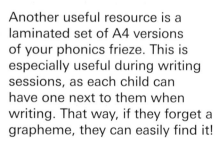

Another useful resource is a laminated set of A4 versions of your phonics frieze. This is especially useful during writing sessions, as each child can have one next to them when writing. That way, if they forget a grapheme, they can easily find it!

Spelling aids

Every classroom throughout the primary school should have word finders available for the children to use when writing. These should contain high-frequency words that are appropriate for their age and ability. It might be helpful for you to have a selection of word finders at different levels for different groups within the class. They should be kept in your literacy area so that they are on hand for the children. As children become independent readers and writers, age-appropriate dictionaries and thesauruses should also be available for them, including (if children have access to computers) the thesaurus on Word. Obviously, a comprehensive computer policy should also be in place.

In our school, we teach keywords that are phonetically irregular as 'red' words. These are taught half-termly from reception to Year 6. After the words have been taught to the children, they are displayed in the classroom on the ceiling above the literacy area so that the children can refer to them when they are writing.

Fingerspace helper

Some children find making fingerspaces between words really easy, and other children find it really, really tricky! Therefore, a fingerspace helper can be useful, particularly for left-handed children. They should be readily available in your literacy corner for children to use if they wish. The idea is that a child uses the laminated finger in their book or on their paper to help them create a space, without the added problem of coordinating their own hands. It is important that the teacher has a giant version to model when demonstrating writing. However, they should also model using a real finger from time to time!

Connectives

We constantly talk about the use of connectives as a way to improve children's writing. Therefore, it is really helpful for the children to have some kind of visual aid to use when writing so that they can explore a range of different connectives. You might make large connectives to hang from the ceiling.

Here, we have made giant jigsaw pieces (a play on the word 'connectives') and display the words on either side. You could even colour-code your connectives according to their purpose, e.g. time connectives in green, location connectives in yellow etc.

Alternatively, you might make a laminated connective prompt board for children to have on their tables when writing. Make sure that the connectives chosen are appropriate for the age and ability of your children.

Punctuation prompts

A punctuation prompt board could be displayed in your classroom for the children to refer to. The display below was created in a Year 6 classroom and is colour-coded yellow, blue and red according to different levels of attainment. Each display also gives an example of how that particular type of punctuation can be used. The children can then check their writing to ensure they have an appropriate range.

If you do not have space for such a display in your classroom, or the display is in a place where it can't be seen by every child, laminated punctuation prompt cards could be provided for children to have on their tables when writing.

49

Maths resources

We have talked about the importance of having a central maths corner in your classroom for all your maths resources, on pages 12–13. In this section, we describe what these might be, and how children can use them to aid their learning.

Multiplication square

In any classroom in Key Stage 2 or upper Key Stage 1, a giant multiplication square is a fantastic tool not only for helping children to learn times tables, but also as a teaching resource for games and five minute fillers. In all our Key Stage 2 classrooms we have created giant, brightly-coloured multiplication boards. These boards are close to the maths corner and accessible to the children, for example, near the classroom carpet area.

Approach

1. Back the board in one colour. Cut out small squares (the size will depend on the board,) and glue on to create a chequered effect. Add large, bright clear numbers and back on alternate colours.

2. Tacky back the board to protect so that the children can use and touch.

3. Add words around the board relating to times tables.

4. Questions could also be added to stimulate children's thinking.

Blue balloon number track

Large, clear number tracks, or progressions, are crucial in any classroom. They can help children with number recognition, counting, number problems, addition and subtraction sums. Number tracks will vary according to children's age. For example, our giant balloon number track runs across the length of our reception classroom and focuses on the numbers 0 to 20. We also have a counting in 2s number track made out of bicycles. In other classrooms you would find number tracks counting in 3s, 5s and 10s or even 100s. Providing access to a variety of numbered and empty number lines is also essential.

Approach

1 Cut out giant-size balloons and invite children to paint them in their own choice of shades of blue.

2 Back each balloon on shiny blue paper. Laminate or paint with mixture of PVA glue and water, so they become rigid.

3 Cut out large white numbers and stick onto the balloons.

4 Display clearly in the classroom.

When creating a giant number track, try and relate the chosen subject to the number sequence. For example, for counting in 2s, bicycles were chosen because they have two wheels.

Whale board

Within a classroom, maths resources can vary from a permanent display which teaches children a set concept, to something that can be used to play a game. The adding and subtracting whale display is situated in the reception classroom and is used to challenge the children's addition and subtraction skills. This resource is interactive as the class teacher regularly changes the questions to ensure the children keep thinking.

Approach

1 Paint a **huge** whale for the centre of the display.

2 Create a title: *Solve the Sums with Wally the Whale*. Cut the letters out of different shades and back on a contrasting colour. We chose blue and red.

3 Cut out blue water drops and add different addition and subtraction calculations, one on each drop. Put the answers on different water drops, to help children solve the calculations. This board could also be used for a matching game.

Numbered cones

Maths resources can either be purchased or pre-made by you, the class teacher. These cones have been bought and are used for an array of exciting and stimulating maths games. For example: split children into groups and give each group a different question such as 4 + 3, 7 − 2, 2 × 4. Blow a whistle to start. The first member of each team should either run or bounce on a spacehopper to the correct cone. The first child to reach the correct cone wins a point! You could also adapt this to put numbers in order, add missing numbers, count in numbers, find number patterns, or practise the four operations: addition, subtraction, multiplication and division.

Giant money and carpet shapes

Giant money is a really useful resource. These 'coins' can be used during whole class carpet sessions. For example, passing the coin around the circle, or sorting money into different values. They can also be used to play games with small groups of children. The fact that they are large and visual makes them a very stimulating resource. However it is important that the children also get to use real money during teaching.

The giant shape carpet tiles have also been made by the class teacher. These tiles were cut out of old pieces of carpet. The teacher enlarged each shape on the photocopier and used these as templates to cut out the shapes from carpet tiles.

Further ideas

Beanstalk months of the year: make a 'months of the year' beanstalk out of large leaves.

Factor feet: the teacher gives the child a card with a number on and the child has to jump on two factors that make that number.

Skittles: the child adds/subtracts/divides/multiplies the numbers on the skittles that they knock over.

Bib attack: the child must find the sum that adds/subtracts/multiplies/divides to make the number on the bib.

53

Teaching in role

Teaching in role is a wonderful strategy for bringing lessons alive. It is a fun way to engage and excite every pupil and can range from being as simple as putting a cloak or a hat on in front of the children, to entering the classroom in full character, complete with costume, face paint and accent!

Professor Wiggins and the daffodils

Approach

At the beginning of the unit of work, the teacher enters the classroom dressed as a scientist holding a daffodil. The teacher tells the class that 'he' is a scientist called Professor Wiggins. (The scientist can, of course, be female!) He explains what a scientist is and that he has come to tell them about this fascinating spring flower. He asks: does anybody recognise it? And he gets children to identify that it is a daffodil. Out of his pocket he pulls labels of parts of plants: petal, stem etc. He asks everyone to help him find them on the daffodil and talks about the functions of each one as he identifies them. He could make them memorable by using actions for each part, such as doing a trumpet action for the trumpet in the centre of the daffodil, or a bee action for the pollen.

Professor Wiggins explains that now the class needs to make a scientific diagram to record their findings. He uses a giant picture of a daffodil and models how to label the parts. Next, he tells the class that they are going to have a closer look at the parts and that they will be dissecting daffodils. This will then be one of the activities during the morning, together with labelling daffodils and daffodil artwork.

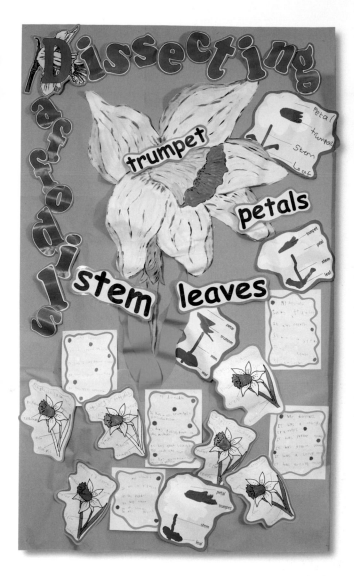

Dissecting daffodils

This is predominantly a science display.

Approach

1   Back the board in pale blue and create a title with letters to spell *Dissecting Daffodils*. Back the D on a daffodil picture.

2   The teacher and groups of children should draw and paint a giant daffodil. Cut out and place in the centre of the display.

3   Label the daffodil parts. Include children's work related to the parts of a daffodil: for example, the children dissected daffodils and stuck the different parts on card, and drew daffodils using a paint package on the computer.

Daffodils

Create a display at the end of the whole unit of work to include a huge range of daffodil artwork.

1   Back the board in pale blue and create lettering in daffodil colours: green, orange and yellow.

2   Make a huge vase to go in the centre of the display out of green and yellow paper and fill with painted daffodils.

3   Include a huge range of artwork including chalk pastel daffodils, textile daffodils, ripped paper daffodils, watercolour daffodils, handprint daffodils and calico daffodils. All the artwork should be backed on daffodil colours.

4   Finish the display by adding keywords related to daffodils.

Further ideas

Other characters for teaching in role include:
*   Queen of shape teaches 2D or 3D shape
*   Count of Number teaches number skills
*   VCOP is a policeman who teaches literacy skills
*   Chef teaches fractions, weight, cooking up a good story/poem etc
*   Word Builder is a builder who teaches word building skills.

The interactive whiteboard

An interactive whiteboard is exciting and offers the possibility of bringing a subject alive. If you use your IWB creatively, and not just as a glorified whiteboard, it will have a huge impact on the quality of teaching and learning in your classroom.

Monet, the interactive artist

The teacher enters the classroom in role as Claude Monet, the famous French artist. He introduces the children to some key facts about himself, e.g. he is an artist, he is French, he draws landscapes, and his passions are light and water. As he talks about these facts, large key words appear on the IWB. He explains to the children that as part of their topic on frogs and ponds he is going to show them some of his famous water lily paintings. Using the IWB, Monet reveals a selection of his works for the children to look at. He discusses with the children how he created his masterpieces and talks through his artistic techniques. With the IWB, you can show large images of Monet's work and zoom in on individual details. Monet reinforces this information about himself and his work by challenging the class to play *True or False*. Words or phrases appear on the IWB and the children must decide if they are true or false. If true, they give Monet a simple thumbs up. If false, they give Monet a thumbs down. He finishes the session by showing his famous painting, *Bridge over a Pool of Water Lilies*, on the IWB, and using chalk pastels he works with the children to make a giant version of his masterpiece. This is then used as part of a Monet display.

A moment with Monet

This display included a huge range of Monet artwork, but the focus was his water lily pictures. The children explored Monet's work in different ways:

- Chalk pastel water lilies on white cartridge paper
- Finger painting water lilies with a collage bridge
- Chalk lilies on black card
- Oil pastel lilies with a blue wash background.

Approach

1 Back the board with blue and create a straight edged border in pink and green paper.

2 Using a computer font print out a title in two shades of green. Staple the children's Monet pictures to one side of the board and the title on the other. Back all the children's work in water lily colours of green, blue and pink, and display.

3 Make a set of words that link to the life of Monet. Back in blue and add to the display.

4 Cut out some small water lily flowers and scatter these over the display.

Further ideas

- **Play Grapes:** using the IWB, create a bunch of grapes. On each 'grape' put letters, numbers, answers to questions etc. The children take it in turns to answer a question by using a plastic fly-swatter to splat the correct answer on the IWB.
- Playing a quiz using IWB (for example, similar to *Who Wants to be a Millionaire*).
- Importing clips of video.
- Using the drawing function of the whiteboard pen.
- Flashing images for children to identify: coins or shapes could spin across the board and children have to identify the correct name.
- Using the spotlight feature to find hidden objects or words.
- Using the magnifying feature to zoom in to examine pictures or text in detail.

The power of games

All children love games! Using games in your classroom makes your lessons lively, fun and dynamic and **perfect** for kinaesthetic learners. There are a huge range of games to explore; we ring the changes and use as many different types as possible.

There are two main kinds:

- Shop-bought games that you can adapt, e.g. *Twister*. Fill the circles with numbers for a lesson on odd and even numbers.

- Games that you make, e.g. a homemade laminated board game about different denominations of money.

Whatever game you are using, it is important to remember:

- **Differentiation:** your game must be appropriate for different ability groups.

- **Relevance:** make sure the game is relevant to your lesson and the learning that is taking place.

- **Quality:** if you are going to the effort of making a game, make sure it is bright, clear, and big. Laminate it so that it will last. If it gets tatty, renew it!

- **Keep it simple.** Make sure the game is easy to learn and that the rules are not too complex!

Fire! Fire!

This game was made as part of a topic on colour and shape. Children were focusing on the colour red and spent two weeks looking at firefighters and fire engines.

Approach

1   Paint and cut out ten large fires and number them 1–10.

2   Make three different sets of fire engines for the class. Set A: with spots for the children to count up to ten. Set B: with simple number pairs to ten. Set C: with three-number bonds to ten.

3   Laminate the fire engines and the fires.

4   **How to play:** place the large fires around the hall, or outdoors.

5   According to ability, give each child a fire engine and ask them to work out the answer. Children with spots would count the spots, children with sums would add using their fingers or mental calculation.

6   The teacher rings a fire bell and the children must run to the correct fire. If a child has six spots on their fire engine, they must run to fire number six. The children sit or stand at the appropriate fire and the teacher checks their answers.

7   Replay over and over again!

Further ideas

We keep a display of game ideas in the staff room. Below we have listed more games for you to try and adapt for your own classroom:

- **Revolving wheel and 'dart' board:** these can be used for teaching addition, subtraction, negative numbers, multiplication, division. The secret of these games is to give each child a whiteboard so all the children can play at once. This will ensure the whole group is involved.

- **Giant bouncers or space hoppers:** these add excitement to a game and also introduce a bit of physical exercise. Children are given a question and they must bounce to the correct answer.

- **Quick-fire mental recall:** the children must pass a ball around the group and recite times tables, alphabetical order, number patterns etc. The child who drops the ball or gets it wrong is OUT!
You can buy resources that add excitement such as *Hot Potato*.

- **Skittles:** you can put anything on the skittles: numbers, letter sounds, words, pictures etc. The object is for children to knock down the correct skittle. For example, if you stick vowels on the skittles (a e i o u), children must pick a picture out of a bag, say, 'cat', and knock down the skittle with the 'a' vowel.

- **Bell game:** the teacher asks a question and the first child to ring the bell and give the right answers gets a point.

- **Blockbusters:** make a blockbuster board. How to play: children play in teams and the object of the game is to cross from one side of the board to the other by answering questions. The answer to each question begins wih a letter on the board chosen by the team.

Using puppets

Puppets are a wonderful way to capture children's attention. However, teachers can be reluctant to use them, feeling that they need to be perfect ventriloquists to carry off a lesson successfully. This is definitely not the case. Watch children engaging with a puppet; they are so absorbed that they won't give you a second glance! However, if you are still concerned, try making your puppet whisper in your ear, so you have to tell the children what s/he is saying.

Approach

1   You can have lots of fun using different puppets in different ways and giving them different personalities.

2   Clever puppets: puppets that teach the children something they are very good at.

3   Not-so-clever puppets: puppets that make mistakes and the children have to help put them right.

4   Naughty puppets: puppets that are badly behaved are lots of fun!

5   Quiet/shy puppets: gentle puppets that need lots of encouragement and often whisper in the teacher's ear.

Cecil the caterpillar

This puppet is used to teach children in our reception class about caterpillars as part of their topic on bugs. It is a fantastic puppet and if you press a button on its bottom, it talks in caterpillar language! The teacher introduces Cecil to the children and explains that she can understand what he is saying. Cecil then tells children lots of facts about caterpillars and the teacher translates, e.g. Cecil says that caterpillars have six legs like other insects, and along the rest of the body are suckers.

Caterpillar display

1   Back the board in pale blue.

2   Make circles in different shades of green and stick letters that spell *Caterpillars* on circles. Arrange the circles on the board so that they look like a caterpillar.

3   Include a range of caterpillar artwork: caterpillars sewn on hessian, potato-print caterpillars, and collage caterpillars. Back caterpillar work on different greens and red backing papers.

Fred Frog

The teacher uses this puppet to teach children in the initial stages of phonic development. Fred the frog is a baby frog who can't talk properly yet. When he speaks he talks purely in sounds, so when you ask his name he says, "F-r-e-d". The children have to blend the sounds together to make 'Fred'. The teacher asks Fred Frog lots of questions, such as, "Where do you live, Fred?" He replies, "P-o-n-d".

Once the children are good at blending the sounds together to make words, they then learn to talk like Fred too, which gives them practice in segmenting words.

Charlie Chicken and Plop the baby barn owl

In our school, these two puppets are used as part of our maths curriculum and the children love them.

Charlie is a clever chicken who is a bit of a know-it-all. He comes to teach the children maths concepts, but is very naughty and unacceptably rude (to the children and the teacher!) and is usually sent out of the classroom before the lesson finishes!

In contrast, Plop the baby barn owl is very shy and quiet. She also visits maths lessons, but isn't very clever as she is still a baby and gets things wrong all the time. The children love her and want to help her, and when she finally gets the answer right, they are over the moon!

Chatting chums

Using chatting chums in the classroom is a good way to maximise children's involvement in the lesson through pair work. Instead of asking children to respond to questions by putting their hands up, the teacher asks them to turn to their chatting chums and discuss the answer. The teacher then chooses a pair to respond. The benefits of using this strategy are enormous:

- It eliminates the problem that some children always put their hand up and some children never do.

- It gives children who might be a bit nervous a chance to discuss their ideas with a partner before talking in front of the class, therefore giving them more confidence.

- It ensures that all children engage in the lesson as the teacher might choose them to respond.

Approach

- **Choosing chatting chums:** generally, it is best to pair a higher ability with a lower ability child. This way, one child can give the other more confidence to offer ideas in front of the class. However, to maximise children's learning, it is also important to consider friendships and personality.

- **Changing chatting chums:** it is important that children have opportunities to work with a variety of partners. Changing chatting chums weekly or fortnightly is appropriate.

- **Managing chatting chums:** introduce a few guidelines to make your carpet sessions run smoothly:

  1 Chatting chums should sit side by side, facing the teacher.

  2 At a pre-arranged start signal, children should turn to face their chatting chums and start chatting!

  3 At the teacher's stop signal, pairs should stop and turn back to face the teacher.

  4 The teacher will then choose a pair or pairs to feed back to the class. The teacher could do this in a number of ways to make it completely random: for example, prepare a pot of lolly sticks with a child's name on each and pull one out to see which pair is chosen.

Using chatting chums

Chatting chums can be used in a variety of ways. In the photo the teacher arrived as the King of Consonants. When a letter appeared on the IWB the children showed green when it was a consonant and red when it was not. Ask each pair to respond to a statement by:

- showing the green side of a paddle if they think it's true, and red if they think it's false

- showing thumbs up or thumbs down

- on a given signal, all calling their answers out at the same time

- displaying the answer on a fan of numbers or letters

- writing the answer on a whiteboard and holding it up

- circling the correct answer/picture on a laminated board and holding it up

- anything else you can think of – be as creative as you like!

Chatting chums display

Approach

1 Create a chequered board by backing a board in white paper. Cut out and stick on yellow squares, 25 cm in size.

2 Create a title using a computer font.

3 Take photos of each child and print them out A5 size. Back the pictures on yellow and blue, and laminate. This will ensure they are durable as you will need to move them around when you change chatting chums. Pair the children and place the pictures together on the board.

4 Print out captions about how to be a good chatting chum. Back on a contrasting colour such as red. Place amongst the children's photos.

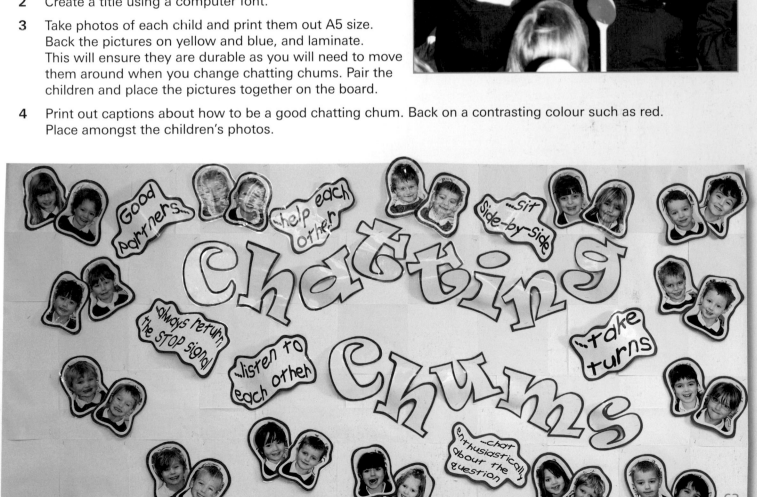

Outside your Classroom

Using the school grounds

Using the entire school environment, indoors and outdoors, is an essential part of classroom practice. School grounds offer huge opportunities for learning, whether or not you are lucky enough to have an environmental area or science garden, a climbing wall or sensory trail, they should be an important and exciting resource for your cross-curricular teaching.

Approach

In this chapter we have used the school grounds to teach about life in Roman times.

- **Carpet session:** Julius Caesar could enter the classroom and demand that his army should get ready to invade Britain. The children would be marched out onto the school field or playground and each given a Roman shield. Throughout the session, Julius Caesar would teach them facts about the Roman army and Roman life.

- **A Roman tour:** A Roman tour guide leads the children around their school and grounds and the children are amazed to find that it has been transformed into a Roman town. (This is done by putting up large images and/or photos. The school pond/swimming pool might be the Roman baths, the school play castle could be the forum, a school assembly area could be an amphitheatre etc.) The tour guide tells the children about each part of a Roman town.

- **The Roman invasion:** This activity uses the school playground, or obstacle course devised by the teacher. In two teams, the children must cross the playground or obstacle course. Each member must answer correctly a question about Roman life, or the Roman army, before they can start. You could also play this game with a climbing wall. If a child puts a foot on the floor, they must start again and answer another question.

- **Roman army training camp:** this is an extension of the carpet session and would take place in the playground or school field. The children would work as a group with Julius Caesar to practise different army formations, e.g. the 'turtle' with shields above their heads.

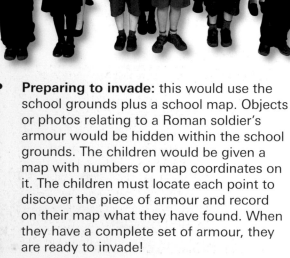

- **Preparing to invade:** this would use the school grounds plus a school map. Objects or photos relating to a Roman soldier's armour would be hidden within the school grounds. The children would be given a map with numbers or map coordinates on it. The children must locate each point to discover the piece of armour and record on their map what they have found. When they have a complete set of armour, they are ready to invade!

A Roman's world

Approach

1 Back the board in blue and create a border in red and gold paper.

2 Encourage the children to chalk pastel a Roman town. Ask small groups to draw and chalk pastel the main landmarks. Add to the display with appropriate labels.

3 Create a title using a Roman-style font. Print out on black paper and back on gold.

4 Print out questions relating to Roman life. Back on red and place around the Roman town. Print out facts about the Romans and place on a Roman temple. Back on gold.

5 Put words relating to the Roman army on a drawing of a Roman soldier. Cut out and back on red. Arrange on the display.

Further ideas

- Ask the children to draw and label a Roman soldier in his uniform.
- After researching shields, ask the children to design their own shield using oil pastels.

65

Using the playground

Every school has a playground and it is important that you make the most of this valuable resource and cater for all kinds of learners. In some schools, year groups have playgrounds solely dedicated to them and it is the teacher's responsibility to set up and organise this space. This can be very exciting and allows for lots of creativity.

Creating a fun and exciting playground

Approach

- **Track for trikes:** lots of playgrounds encourage young children to use their gross motor skills by providing trikes to ride. These can dominate a playground and prove difficult to manage, so create a road for the children to follow. Include stop signs and a zebra crossing.

- **Remember role play:** create an area which is dedicated to role play, include costumes for the children to wear and things for them to do by providing props (see page 70 for more detail).

- **Co-operative toys:** encouraging children to play together is a part of school life. Including co-operative toys such as a seesaw, bat and ball, two- and three-seater trikes etc develops children's social skills massively.

- **Table-top activities:** these give less-active children an engaging playtime. Writing activities, reading books, and small world activities such as a farm or dolls' house can all add to a fun playtime.

- **Construction carpet:** many children love to build and make things. A construction carpet ensures that they have space to build and use their creations.

- **Adventure trail:** anything that encourages children to develop their gross motor skills is an excellent resource. A mini-adventure trail is a good way to make physical exercise available in your playground area.

- **Caterpillar Corner:** adding a bit of quirkiness to a playground can turn a good playground into a very good playground. Create special areas for the children to play such as Caterpillar Corner.

Using the playground to enhance teaching for learning

It is really important that your playground is not just for playtime but is a resource you can use at any time and for any lesson.

Playground markings: most playgrounds have markings that can be used for classroom activities. At our school we have deliberately designed our playground in this way. This is great for your kinaesthetic learners and adds a little bit of fun to the lesson:

- Alphabet Bubbles or Alphabet Grid: jump or throw bean bags on the letters to spell words.

- Number Snake or Hopscotch: throw bean bags and use the numbers to add, subtract, multiply and make new numbers.

- Number Basket: throw bean bags, bounce, or jump to develop numeracy skills.

Playground areas: playgrounds can be split into areas to include a boat or an adventure trail. These will add a different dimension to your teaching:

- Pirate Ship can be used as a role-play area.

- Percussion Playground can be used during a music lesson or to create sounds for stories or to help spell out words during a syllable lesson.

- Giant Maze is great fun for hiding clues, letters, number objects etc for children to collect.

- An adventure trail can be used to add a challenge to a lesson. Place questions along the trail for the children to answer.

67

Independent play

Many infant classrooms have a separate area for independent play. This area might be inside the classroom or outside in a covered area, but the aim is the same: to provide children with opportunities for independent play focused on activities that encourage learning in all areas of the curriculum.

The key to providing rich opportunities for play is **variety**. Activities should be carefully designed so that they:

- appeal to boys and girls
- cater for different interests and promote different kinds of learning, e.g. writing activities, art activities, construction, small world toys, sand and water play etc. Even furniture adds a varied dimension: activities on mats on the floor, on tables, activities to stand at, and cushions to sit on.

Independent play ideas

- **Sand play:** provide different toys for wet and dry sand. For wet sand, use moulds, buckets and tools. When the sand is dry, provide buckets, jugs, funnels, sieves and sand wheels. Encourage children to use appropriate vocabulary to describe the sand as they play.

- **Water play:** change the toys in the water tray so that children play with the water in different ways. On one day you might provide a range of jugs, funnels, tubes, pumps, pipettes, and waterwheels. The next day you might put out toys that float and sink and on the following day, a magnetic fishing set. You might even change the focus of your sand or water tray to support other learning in the classroom, e.g. if you are learning about penguins, float polystyrene in the water tray to represent icebergs and provide penguin small world toys!

- **Writing table:** an exciting range of resources is key to encouraging children to put pen to paper. Provide clearly labelled zippy bags of coloured paper, paper and envelopes. Pencils, crayons, pens, felt-tips, chalks, glue sticks and scissors should also be easily accessible. Display current topic-related words close to the writing table, so that children can use them if they want to. A post box encourages children to post letters.

  Change your writing table from time to time to add interest, e.g. when reading *We're going on a Bear Hunt*, put the writing table inside a bear's cave and encourage the children to write letters to the bear by torchlight!

- **Construction:** vary your construction corner on different days to get children to use different skills: e.g. one day put out Lego, Duplo and giant bricks, but on another day put out construction kits with wheels, or stickle bricks. Put out paper and pencils to help children to plan their models or draw the finished product. Provide an area where children can display their finished models and provide cards on which they can write labels or captions to describe them.

- **Small world:** small world play is all about imagination! Small world toys can be made even more exciting by giving children the resources to create an environment. For example, with dinosaurs you could also put out a dinosaur mat, potted plants, sand, twigs, leaves, chip bark etc so children can create their own realistic jungle scene!

- **Art and craft:** children love to repeat things on their own that they have done in the classroom with their teacher! Once you have taught a skill in the classroom, put the same resources in the play area and see what the children come up with. If you have used potatoes to print a caterpillar in the classroom, on the next day provide potatoes, paints and a range of other things that they might use to print with in the play area.

- **Investigative activities:** provide a range of resources that will encourage children to explore and develop their understanding of the world. For example, you might put out a range of magnets together with magnetic and non-magnetic materials, or, after learning how to make an electrical circuit in the classroom, provide batteries, wires, crocodile clips, bulbs, buzzers and switches for them to experiment with in their play.

- **Large scale activities:** use the playground or a large space to put on activities on a LARGE SCALE! Stick sheets of giant paper together and provide paint and letter sponges for the children to print letters and words. Another idea is to put your water tray outside and use large bits of guttering and buckets etc to create a giant water world!

- **Cross-curricular activities:** if children particularly enjoyed a theme or topic in the classroom, use this interest to stimulate their independent play. For example, when learning about Elmer the Elephant, plan independent play activities using the story.

You could set up the puppet theatre with jungle animals and an Elmer puppet, using a jungle small world. Provide elephant pictures and multi-coloured paper and encourage children to draw Elmer's patchwork squares, or cut out and stick a patchwork elephant etc.

The best thing about independent play is there are no limits. Use your imagination… and **have fun!**

Role-play areas

Role-play areas are an important feature of reception and Key Stage 1 classrooms, but could also be a wonderful addition to older classrooms, too. Role play offers fantastic opportunities for developing speaking and listening skills, improving confidence and reading and writing in a play situation.

When developing a role-play area, it is good practice to make links between this and other areas of the curriculum. For example, when learning about money, set up a shop as a role-play area, or when learning about pirates, set up a pirate ship and a desert island.

It is also important to invent as many roles as possible for the children to act out and provide appropriate costumes, props and ideas. If children have never used a role-play area before, it is helpful to have an adult working with children to show them the kind of things they can do. To make this really exciting the teacher him/herself could go into role. For example, when opening a building site the teacher might take on the role of the foreman, or when opening Willy Wonka's chocolate factory, the teacher might be Willy Wonka him/herself and give each child a golden ticket.

The Jolly Post Office

This role play area was set up to complement the children's literacy work on the story, *The Jolly Postman*. It is particularly good for developing letter-writing skills and reading.

Approach

1   Cut out a set of red letters to say, *Jolly Post Office* and back on blue (post office colours).

2   Set up the inside of the role-play area as a 'sorting office'. Make boxes and write on them the names and addresses of characters from the story.

3   Make a similar set of laminated envelopes which include names and addresses and a stamp and postmark. The children can then work in here as 'sorters', reading the addresses and sorting the envelopes into the boxes.

4   Set up a table and chair as a post office counter. Include a till, boxes with laminated 1st class and 2nd class stamps and a set of weighing scales. The post office counter clerk can work here, selling stamps to the customers.

5   Set up a writing table and post box. Display the characters from the story's names and addresses, and provide paper and envelopes. The children can then write letters to the characters, buy a stamp and post their letter in the post box.

6   Finally, provide costumes for the children. You should include costumes, badges, and props for a variety of roles: Jolly Postman, post office counter clerk, sorters, characters from the story to be the customers, e.g. Cinderella, three bears etc.

Dilly's Garden Centre

This role-play area was set up to complement the children's maths work on money. The class teacher came into the classroom in role as a character called Dilly, who wanted to set up a garden centre because she loved flowers, but didn't have a clue about money! Over a series of lessons, children taught her about coin recognition, adding money and giving change, and as part of every lesson the children worked in small groups on the till in Dilly's garden centre.

Further ideas

Other ideas for role-play areas might include:

- a fire station to support work on 'People who help us'
- Santa's grotto at Christmas time
- a Creepy Crawly Café to support work on minibeasts
- a safari camp to support work on African animals
- a travel agency to support geography work
- a French café to support Key Stage 2 work on food
- a bike shop to support work on vehicles.